Hello from the Wreckage

By Fadi Yousef

Published by Metaphysical Fox Press
roberteugeneperry@gmail.com

Copyright © 2025
Fadi Yousef &
Metaphysical Fox Press

All Rights Reserved
ISBN# 9798284284919
Cover design Susan R Scott & Fadi Yousef

Metaphysical Fox Press asks that no part of this publication be reproduced or transmitted in any form for profit by any means electronic or mechanical, including photocopy, recording or information storage or retrieval system without permission in writing from Metaphysical Fox Press.
This is to help support the publisher and the artists.

Dedicated to Saint Mary's Syriac Orthodox Church

Table of Contents

Yes They Came
....
13

Hello From the Wreckage
....
15

Love's Rush Hour
....
16

Learning How to Write
....
17

Bunch of Jokers
....
19

Summing Up My Day
....
20

Heart to Heart Conversation
....
21

An Arresting Dream
....
22

Doors
....
23

Rear View Mirror
....
25

Thresholds

26

Overdue Sun

28

Shipwrecked

29

The Beauty Pageant

30

Quenching the Shadows

31

Miles Gathering

32

Snowing in Heaven

33

Word of Mouth

34

Welcome

35

Tip Toeing the Night

36

The World's Appetite

37

Planting a Kiss
....
38

Am
....
39

Destinations
....
41

Reflecting on the Self
....
42

School Closed for Snow Day
....
43

Crime of Passion
....
44

Mating with a Poem
....
45

Cutting Through
....
46

Diving In
....
47

Not For Sale
....
48

Postcard
....
50

Ashes

51

The Burglar

53

Promises of Ghettos

54

Mother Nature

55

What Remains

56

Nature Reflects

58

Journey to Remember When

60

Flower's Currency

62

All in the Timing

63

Waiting to Go Home

64

Our Daily Bread

65

Links of Hope

66

The Art of Thievery

67

A Love Letter From Mother Nature

68

Blood in the Rain

69

Weeding Out the Tears

71

Devil's Whiskers

72

Dead End Moment

73

Step for Step

74

The Earthquake

75

Crystal Ball

76

Shards of the Future

77

The Cornerstone
....
78

An Arresting Dream
....
79

Fishing
....
80

Hormones of Morning
....
81

Closet Where Seasons Keep Their Junk
....
82

Rubble of Dreams
....
83

Blind Date
....
84

A Man's Hands
....
85

A Woman's Hands
....
87

Water's Journey
....
89

Heaven To Look Forward To
....
91

Gears of Loss

92

Winter Worries

93

Haiku 1

94

Haiku 2

94

Haiku 3

94

Haiku 4

94

Haiku 5

94

Haiku 6

95

Haiku 7

95

Haiku 8

95

Haiku 9

95

Haiku 10

....

95

Haiku 11

....

96

Haiku 12

....

96

Haiku 13

....

96

Haiku 14

....

96

Haiku 15

....

96

Haiku 16

....

97

Haiku 17

....

97

Haiku 18

....

97

Haiku 19

....

97

Haiku 20

....

97

Haiku 21

98

Haiku 22

98

Haiku 23

98

Yes They Came

Yes they came
For the bulgur wheat and lentils
The feta cheese and Alfonso olives
Paprika nutmeg and cloves
But what they really came for
Was his charcuterie board of wisdom
And his faithful words
Which were the real spice of life
Everything imported
From years of struggle
When we immigrated from dry dirt
Where only war grows
From a Middle East
And its whirlpool of religions
To the U.S. and its
Promising soil
Where father sowed his children

On rainy days the customers shuffled in
Complaining about the weather
He would say
"You have to drink water don't you "
But father's words became watered down
Competition opened up in the city
Kind of like a holy war
Of Mediterranean stores
Each pitching their edible propaganda
As the sales slowed down
Like a rolling coin that wobbled
And fell to a halt

And in the end

The moths and gnats got into everything
Chewing and biting
Through the bags and bread
Leaving father with a mouthful of words
He never got to say

And as he got sick
They couldn't get all the fluids out
And he checked out of this world
Without a receipt to look back
And I was stuck
Tending the market without a vision
My soul on sale for a moment of time
To jot down a poem
A square peg
Trying to fit into a round hole
A bull in a China shop
Of fine ideas

As on the last day of business
A pigeon not minding its own
Flew in past the door
Crashing into the glass window
Shopping for a blue sky
Where father now walked the aisles

Hello From the Wreckage

Forgot her number
Dial all the possibilities to her voice
Try to crack the code
To her laugh
As I try pushing
Her infinite buttons
To get a reaction
Random as the stars
Illogical as the
Freckles on her face
Just a matter of wiring
In the mindless circuits
Of space and distance
Learning how to say
"Wrong number"
In so many moods and languages
As I am outnumbered
By my hopscotching frustration
Until I miraculously
Reach the dial tone
Of your heart
Like cracking the safe
To your love
As I hold you so close
To my cheek
Hear you whisper
In my ear
Feel the operator of your soul
Smiling

Love's Rush Hour

Open my eyes
Throw the covers off the sun
Leave the imprint of a dream
On the pillow
Get down on my knees
To prey on night's ghosts
That might have followed me
Shower away the stars
Stuck in my hair
Brush the teeth
That took a bite of stale darkness
Pick out a suit
Well suited for my mood
With a tie like a bow
To present the gift I am
To the world
As my senses are unwrapped
By the scent of coffee
Another day in the air
And her smile in the kitchen
Spreading faster than the light
As I face the rush hour
Of your love

Learning How to Write

He told me
That in order to learn
How to write
I must visit museum wings
And let my imagination take flight
And read lots of poetry books
To reach closure
With dead poets
And the afterlife of their work
And take long walks
In the woods
Studying the different seasons
Of shadows
Hunting the camouflaged silence

But I told him
My pen is homeless
My ghosts walks down streets
Between a poem's lines
Turning the corners of line breaks
Picking up cans
And cannots
Paying my dues
To the day's author
And learning the do nots
Of unknotting a poem

Between stanzas of brick
I am the rhythmic mortar
Scribbling graffiti on walls of books
Before the day turns the cover
Like an editor of the crumbling light

As I am unattached
No heir to literature's
Crown of the past
Just following the lineage
Of the next cursive wind
That signs the air

Bunch of Jokers

Bunch of jokers
Sat down to poker
To gamble the night away

The moonlight was ample
As they began to gamble
Bluffing their drunkenness away

One with a flush
Betting in a rush
As his face turned to stone

The other with a full house
Staying silent as a mouse
His losses he must atone

As chips take flight
Each thinking they're right
In their minds assured

And cards are flipped over
And eyes begin to hover
Curiosity cured

One disappointed
As the chips are counted
And debts are settled

One thing learned
Between the victor and the burned
Is with Lady Luck you never meddle

Summing Up My Day

An algorithm of birds
An algebraic equation
Whose beauty can't be solved
All pecking under
The right angle of sunlight
The chords of rain
Having softened the surface area
Of the plane of earth
Where a constant of worms
Feeds hunger's variable
And dew twinkles
Exponentially in prisms
As wings multiply
Into the air
And gravity is subtracted
By a soaring wind
As clouds divide into zero
Equally in the sky
And nature blooms
Without math or proof
Into the infinite day
Adding a shape shifting smile
To my face
As I try to sum up
The pi of Mother Nature's miracle
Running out of fingers

Heart to Heart Conversation

It starts with a "good morning"
Dreamy words
That have found the light
At the end of sleep's tunnel
Stowed away in the death of night
To the afterlife of day
Where many voices rise
With the all the tones of the sun

As the first syllables of dawn
Leave the horizon's lips
Kissing the moon goodbye
The darkness filtering
Into a black coffee
Sugared by your sweet eyes
Where I find my dialogue
As we cut each other off
In love's mid sentence
Your hand speechless
On my shoulder
Curving the silence carefully
As I buy time with a smile
Purchasing your rich verbs of passion
And I kiss you with
All the adjectives I know
Until I become fluent
In man's first romance language
An ancient dialect
Only the heart knows
As we communicate
Mouth to mouth
Stealing the words
At the tip of your tongue

An Arresting Dream

Dawn
Simple as dew
Complex as
A conversation about a dream
But what did you really see there
Between the loose ends of sleep
That tied you up in knots
To unravel in an early morning talk
With a lover
Unpacking your words
And all their luggage
Into a cup of coffee
Having crossed the borders of night
Into the safe checkpoint of his arms
His eyes patting you down
From the sharp worries of the world
That may prick your love
As his arresting smile
Handcuffs the darkness
Finding you guilty of innocence
And sentences you
To a lifetime
Behind bars of his love poems

Doors

My brother and I decided
To play a joke on our other brother
We called upstairs
And told him
Charbel we found another door
He was busy studying
All the pathways to success
But he rushed down to the market
And asked our father
Dad? Is there really another door?
We all broke out
In bent over knee slapping laughter

It was good for the moment
But the moments turned into years
And we all found our doors
Some that led to family and success
Some to darkness
Where I felt around
Bumping my knee
On the devil's prayer mat
Which unlocked the cell
To drug abuse and mental illness
Where no light shined
On the mind
And no window to reality
As the bars closed on innocence
My youth sentenced to years
Of shaming the family
And humiliating our name
Like a branch that broke off
From the family tree

And grafted onto nameless weeds
Where I was stepped on by the years
As I tried to grow through the cracks
Fighting the gravitational pull
Of an unworldly love

But it wasn't till I found my roots
That I began to bloom
Photosynthesized by my family's light
Watered by tears
Running down the face of time
Sheltered under wings
Of many an angel
As I slowly feathered
Back into society

Where even I found the door
My family had left ajar
In case one day
I find the key to life

Rear View Mirror

I have this feeling
That I'm gonna die on the highway
Not for speeding through life
But for going too slow
No wife and kids
No one to share the steering wheel with
No one to keep warm
The engine of my heart
As I sometimes hitchhike
Through the streets of loneliness
Or drive through insecurity
Windshield smudged
With deluded visions
The radio playing
The soundtrack of my despair
As I connect the white lines
Of destiny
That perforate
As soon as I pass them
A bridge of broken promises
Crumbling behind me
Like taking advantage
Of fuel for just a moment
Sparking the next mile
Before I am spit out
Like smoke that disappears
Without leaving a trace
That I was even there
Until I am maybe remembered
By death's rear view mirror

Thresholds

They walk they crawl
Cane step and carried
Through the doors
Dressed in the ironed Sunday sunlight
As frankincense fills the temple
Of their bodies
And their pride takes a knee
On the plush runner
That runs away
With their worries
As they practice a faith
Immigrated but not assimilated
By one word or tradition
That they carried on their backs
Over oceans and waves of discrimination

The priest too
Smuggled over without blemish
To his holiness
On his tongue the ancient language
Of Aramaic
Shared only in a heart to heart
By very few people
Trickled down through the generations
Without losing a drop of holy water
That quenches the thirst of believers

As they sit down
On the many pews
Like tween the ribs of the Lord
Getting comfortable in God's lap

As stained glass windows
Breathe in the light
Images shining through the ages
To reach the sacred altar
That holds up the weight of the world
Where sin is ripped apart like bread
And miraculously disappears
Into the nooks and crannies
Of the Holy Eucharist
As our faith turns to crumbs
With which we feed the world

Overdue Sun

Intentions to go writing at the park
But the rain punctuates the day
One long run on sentence
Without a period of rest

As I rephrase my plans
And stay inside with you
Under the sunshine
Of the lamp in the bedroom
Our bodies energized
With enough wattage
To light our world
Under the covers
As ecstasy flickers on and off
For so many hours
The sweat short circuiting
At our fingertips
Until we burn out

And the rainstorm reaches
It's last chapter
The lightning in bold print
The thunder stealing the ending
As Mother Nature archives
The day's story on a shelf
In a library always growing
Past the bookends

As the overdue sun
Pays its late fee to the darkness
And borrows tomorrow's book

Shipwrecked

What are you hiding
Behind that coy smile
Are you the thief of the hours
The robber of innocence
My mother told me about
When I hid behind the curtain
Of her dress
Are you the boogie man
Masked behind perfume
Do your pockets hold
Coined phrases of lost love
Is heartbreak the currency
With which you barter
For a young man's soul
A glance hooked on a line
With bated breath
Fishing for short affairs
To throw back in the sea
Never taking me ashore
To learn your secrets
Spilled in waves
As one by one
The tide of years ebb
But my memories
Still drown in your eyes
Even though my hopes
Are shipwrecked in stormy waters
As I realize
That I will always be vainly sailing
Towards the bay of your arms

The Beauty Pageant

The beauty of beauty pageants
Where judges critique curves
On the palate of the mind
God's latest creation on stage
Where symmetry is prized
Unlike the awe of Mother Earth
That grows wild
Naked mountains and valleys
That have never been awarded
Taken for granted
In contesting ages
As a country from every geography
Struts its stuff
Born from time's high heels
And a woman is favored
For how her curves hug the globe
As she is crowned with applause
And flowered with smiles
As she enjoys fame
Shorter than a falling tear
Before the earth takes back
The beauty that belongs to it

Quenching the Shadows

The bubbling fountain
Wets the morning's appetite
For hummingbirds and squirrels
Chasing their thirst and hunger
That's never fully caught
In the net of days
Like water that never takes shape
Unless it dies in a freeze
And reincarnates into tears
Or a wagon wheel that never
Reaches its destination
Always spinning
Without destiny
As the world turns in space
But nothing moves on earth
And I am grounded in the courtyard
Counting the hours in a moment
Where the winged light
Never lands long enough
To quench the shadows

Miles Gathering

You promised
We would age together
Wink at the days and their visions
As they went by
And laugh at the darkness
When we wined
And the fire waned

But death put out your spark
And I was left to burn
My soul the log
Fueling my loneliness
As the flames split and rejoined
Like our hands on your deathbed
And I learned to let go of the warmth
We are all born with
Forgetting the degrees of separation
Between two bodies
As I face your grave memories
That I can never bury
Stored in a plot in the mind
That flower to life everyday
When my thoughts pace long enough
One way into the past
And the miles between us
Gather

Snowing in Heaven

It's c c cold
Six degrees of separation
Between me and your warm arms
As icicles like bones
Hold up the body of winter
And cells of snow
Begin to fall
Covering the skeletal season
As I stare out from eyes
Hollow with loneliness
Tracing a flake
In its midlife crisis like me
Being just a snowman
With no spring in his step
Who will soon face the sun
And melt into the years
With no guts to face the ages
Leaving behind stones
That were once a smile
Now frowning at death
And eyes of charcoal
Turned to diamonds
Under the pressure of life's visions
As I engage the afterlife
Marrying flesh and spirit
Where I mingle like a snowflake
Never to be grounded again

Word of Mouth

Since the beginning of time
When words were still lost on lips
There have been recorders
Of life's beauty
Hunted and gathered
And found scribbled on rock
Or etched in the mind
Until we turn the page
To today's scavengers of the word
Where authors prey on one another
And readers burn books
To keep their ignorance warm
As an idea is born
From a virgin muse
Suckling from the teat
Of imagination
Crying for a page
To breathe
As the pen quickly kisses paper
Giving mouth to mouth to the thought
That comes to life in a book
With its numbered days

Welcome

Thin coating of snow
The earth below moves like a snake
Before molting its skin in the sun
Hissing as heat dissipates
And disappears
Funny how in the wild
One thing depends on another
And Mother Nature has a recipe
For each day's nurturing
And every creature and plant
Is an ingredient
For life and death
As I look out into the field
Wonder how the past seeds the future
How many links in the food chain
That never rust in the rain
Or break under the pressure of the years
Wonder how many lives
Rely on me
And how I rely
On the web of the world
That spiders in all directions
As I place a welcome mat at my door
To keep an open mind

Tip Toeing the Night

Taking a night walk
Just tip toeing through the stars
Chasing the tomorrow
That hides behind the moon
My steps soft as
The velvet darkness
That conceals the mystery
Of a black cat and
Its tiny headlights
Going the wrong way
Down a one way street
Where it meets in patches
With the moonlight lost too
Asking for directions
As I let it shine
Carrying the light on my face
Lead it out
And with my finger
Trace its way home
Before the dawn begins to purr

The World's Appetite

A seed of wheat
Such a small thing
Bursting with life
That will soon feed the world
A miracle
Of mathematical wonder
Growing exponentially
Solving hunger
With roots reaching down
To the waters of hope
And a golden head
Praying in the sun
For a graceful harvest
As they grow without witness
Quietly curing famine
Feeding the crop
Of open mouths
Never taking a bite
For its own appetite
Only worries about
The empty stomach of silos
As a wind blows
And they wave to me
In my full loneliness
The wind stalking the field
With a dream about a grain
In a hungry breeze

Planting a Kiss

Your neck
The frontier of your beauty
Where I war with myself
To touch
Or only to look
Disturb such a specimen
Behind the glass of sleep
Your soul perusing
A museum of dreams
Studying all the works of art
Of your self portrait
As I take in
The masterpieces of your breaths
Against the white canvas pillow
Your smile of comfort
Brushing me away
As my imagination
Paints a picture of where you are
A vision of you
In love's orchard
Picking passion fruit
To share with me
As the pit of your eyes open
Harvesting the daylight
And I plant the right unspoken words
With a kiss on your lips

Am

I am weak
When the beauty of the sun
Stretches its muscles at dawn
I am strong
When your smile lifts
The weight of the world
I am lonely
When the distance between us
Holds my hand
I feel pain
When your needling words
Prick my trust
I feel joy
When I celebrate the Holy days
At the altar of your name
I age
Only to grow young
In the fountain of your eyes
I do not speak
Lest I mispronounce our love
So just hold me
And let the moonlight
Fine tune the night
Let the song of our passion
Play over and over again
As the lyrics of ecstasy
Record in our hearts
Your screams topping the charts
As my finger writes music
On sheets of your white skin
The words taken from my lips
To your lips

As I give mouth to mouth
To the dying darkness
That has already begun to hum
Morning's melody

Destinations

Frost on my windshield
You yelling from the passenger seat
Can't see where I'm going
What if I take a wrong turn
In our relationship
And get pulled over
By heartbreak
Or down love's one way road
With no turning back
Our wheels just spinning
In the quicksand of drama
Always leading
To a dead end
As our words
Run out of gas
And into silence
Where our eyes like spark plugs
Ignite into passion
And we idle in a kiss
My hands steering
From your hips to your shoulders
As your ecstasy
Blindsides the night
And we face the realization
That we've reached
The destination we were looking for

Reflecting on the Self

Talking to myself
In front of the mirror
A glass lake
That reflects my words
Questions rippling back
About how I look
A three piece suit
Looking tenfold dapper
As a breeze comes ashore
Waving my hair back
As I comb for wrinkles
In my garment
And straighten out my smile
That emerges from
The edge of my happiness
My penny loafers
Making plenty sense
Maybe to barter
For a woman's look
As I step away
From the mirror... my momentary mistress
Who never says no
To an affair

School Closed for Snow Day

Kids like snowflakes liberated
One from the doors of heaven
The other from behind book covers
As freedom educates the neighborhood
In the science of happiness
The math of laughter
The biology of a smile
The history of being young again
And the Shakespearean romance
Of a snowman and snow angel
Still falling in love
As flurries fill the air
Like school bells ringing
In the hallways of the sky
With no time for teachers
To shovel their facts
As I mold my joy
Into a perfect snowball
And aim at the cruel imperfections of time
That have aged my jubilation
Slowly releasing the day
That had targeted my delight
The night beginning to reign
And daylight beginning to melt
As we all go inside
Subjecting ourselves again
To the homework of civility
To study what tomorrow has to offer
To be ready for the morning sun's
Pop up quiz

Crime of Passion

I'm going home
The road shortening
And the past growing
Like a vision of you
With open doors and open arms
As you wait
The night closing in
The darkness sparking
The fireplace
Two empty wine glasses
Filled with moonlight
Where the flames will write our names
In cursive
And we will leave our signature
In the stars
As my steps quicken
Chasing the smoke in the distance
My misery turning to ashes
As I reach the fire
In your eyes
And you ignite my heart
Like love's arsonist
A crime of passion
Sentencing you to a lifetime
In my arms

Mating with a Poem

I threw away a poetry book
A title not entitled to my time
But it opened its covers
And flew away
Spitefully leaving its words
In the sky…. A trail of letters falling
Like black snow flurries
Writing their own
Climactic ending
Landing without rhyme or reason
Into a blank canvas on my mind
As my muse shovels the flakes
With new poems on its metal lips
My imagination snowballing
Into rhythmic order
As my pencil melts
On a page white as winter
Where the verses fall
Like a blizzard of inspiration
And I snowdrift
Into a thought about spring
That will author rebirth
From nature's writer's block
Where my poem will be pollinated
By readers searching to mate
With the many seasons
Of themselves

Cutting Through

Chopping wood
To enjoy the relationship of winter
My axe lost
At the edge of morning
The blade of the cold
Getting a handle on me
As I cut through the sunlight
Divorcing the tree rings
From the past
That had engaged
In a summer's shade
Shadows now frozen
To the hip of a nude maple tree
That gives its limbs
To keep ours warm
Branches always reaching for the sky
To catch the flickering stars of the flames
As they burn through the seasons
To reincarnate in the fireplace
And we fill Mother Nature's ashes
Into an urn on the mantle
Its roots having earned and budded
A place in our memories
To bloom

Diving In

On vacation
On a hammock swinging
Between sunrise and sunset
As afternoon cracks into evening
And I find myself sipping on a coconut
Where I split my time
Between Neruda and Gibran
And I become well versed
In relaxation
Writing a few words of my own
In the disappearing sand
The waves swallowing my lines
Into their fathomless imagination
The moon pulling rhythmically
On the ebb and flow of my rhymes
Read back to me in braille
When my muse becomes beached
And the waters foam at the mouth
Spilling out a drunk message in a bottle
To uncork the night
And unbottle my spirits
And dive into the ocean
To discover all the secret islands
Of the self

Not For Sale

Money can't buy things
Like your love
My heart of gold in my pocket
Jingling like cents from above

And you can't buy Mother Nature
With her many personalities
The eye of the storm
We weather face to face
And the calm of dawn
Where shine all our names

Can't buy health
As our blood ages
And rumors circulate
Like an undying wind in our faces

Can't buy faith
It's something you practice on your knees
Your eyes looking out
Your soul looking in
Praying the days
Don't prey and tease

Can't buy happiness
It's not on any shelf
It's always out of stock
When thinking only of the self

Money can't buy
Real emotion
Like wetting your feet

By the sands of the ocean

Can't even buy
A poem that fully rhymes
My imagination can't be bought
With so many nickels and dimes

The only thing
Money can buy
Is the currency of greed
And loneliness stacked high

Postcard

From my visit to Paris
I take a cross section of the scenery
And send it as a postcard
Stamped with the scents
Of promiscuous women in alleyways
Sending their love
As rats stare at me
From dead ends with beady eyes
As if I was a street exhibit
Of the Louvre gutted inside out
And I walk around freely
Without a ticket to the wonder
Of artists and poets thieving
The living masterpieces of the city
Canvassing and brushing up
On her romance language
Leaving a rudeness
That doesn't translate well
As I too start stealing
With clicks of my camera
For my museum above the fireplace
To keep my memories warm
But as they say
C'est la vie

Ashes

That ticking nicotine clock goes off
The boss of everything I do
That never gives me a break
So I punch out of life for a bit
Grabbing my cancer kit
To have a talk with the Marlboro man
Who never gets off his high horse
Always whipping me with his crop
In a race with a tragic ending
As my heart perpetually breaks
In a love hate romance that can't breathe
As he never talks too much about himself
Always putting his burning words
In my mouth
About the future and reproducing
Offspring with the same habit
To carry forward the brand name
As he blinds me and never
Lets the curtain of smoke rise from my eyes
In a relationship without end
As he always gets angry
When I mention breaking up
Telling him I can no longer trust
This toxic relationship
As he gets emotional
Talking about all the good times we had
And how well gallop into a sure horizon
Making promises that
He'll try to live a bit healthier
And not be so needy
And that he's just like any other
Living thing that God put on earth

As I grab his lying words from the root
And match them to my lips
For one last kiss
Before burying him
In his own ashes

The Burglar

He breaks through a window of time
When the homeowners are away
Hopscotching through the patches of silence
And tiptoeing through the eyes
Of family pictures watching him
As he bumps his toe
At the foot of the bed
Heading straight for her jewelry box
Where the couple hide
The proof of their love
As he lifts the lid of darkness
Revealing her heart of gold
That skips a beat when
Transplanted red handed to his
Also palming
A diamond necklace shining
Like a newly discovered constellation
Never worn out by a stare
Where visions of broaches blind him
Pinned to the chest of night
Accented by earrings listening
Like a witness to the crime
As the moonlight shines
Through the window
Handcuffing his conscience
And he leaves empty handed
Only guilty of stealing
Pearls of sweat

Promises of Ghettos

The many promises of ghettos
Graffitied on its walls
Like the guts of the city
Worn on the outside
As rats sneak around and over
And under brand new sneakers
Copped by sneaking around
Selling bliss in tiny baggies
Wearing baggy pants on corners
Held down by gang colors
Promising a shade of belonging
As rough times tick tock
On expensive watches
Passing by like a drive by
Emptying itself from a cheap revolver
As the earth revolves
With the innocence of youth
Searching for a truth
No longer to be found
At the end of a gun
That fires
But keeps no one warm
As we all chase the high
Of a ghetto's promise

Mother Nature

Dear Mother Nature
The first time we met
I was but a child
Coming up from the horizon
Of mother's arms
And my eyes gave suck
From the teat of your awe
You… you were an old woman
Who birthed my wonder
In the world
Your curves and valleys
Where my eyes belonged
But I was not homeless
Without four walls
Housed and welcomed
By your four elements
Made myself comfortable
In the lap of your wilderness
From where my dreams blow
In the hair of your winds
And my imagination flows
In your rivers and oceans
Like masterpieces hung
On a natural museum turned inside out
Where the Creator perfects his craft
Brushing the world
With a begotten breeze
His mind never going blank
As he brainstorms another day
Brainwashing us with another miracle
Another anonymous breath
That dies to give us life

What Remains

What remains
When the moment is absorbed
Into the day plain
And the darkness lords

And moonlight appears
Poured by the moon
As I sleep with my tears
Over a distant lover swoon

To touch in a dream
So near so far
Possible it seems
Wherever you are

In the recesses of
Somebody's arms
Tossed away love
Though me you harmed

Now again I say
What remains
When the only thing to stay
Is loneliness's fame

So I imagine
Seeing you again
Can I ask your love
Where it has been

And can I follow you home
Without your consent

Like your shadow roam
Until I am spent

Maybe then
It will be fine
To join where we been
And cross that line

And together we can ask
What remains
When two hearts away cast
The questioning chains

What remains are the eyes
Mine and yours
Who have searched the skies
To break down passion's locked doors

Nature Reflects

The day awakens
And the dawn begins to yawn
The sun stretches it rays
On the back of a fawn

Reflects a morning voice
Calling me to the meadow
And so I harken from a dream
A curious fellow

It's the voice of nature
From the bellows of earth
Calling me to witness
The day's birth

I follow my eyes
That unwrap the wonder
As my feet unravel deeper
Into the quiet's thunder

A slow storm
Beginning to take hold
Of bird calls and such
As twilight's mysteries unfold

Untold secrets between
The flowers and bees
Making natural love
In a gentle tease

As continue to open
The petals of wilderness

Blooming like a child
Innocent from man's sins

Worn down I sit upon a rock
In a madness of the senses
No boundaries or limits
Or a vision's fences

Time stopped
No future or past
Only the present
Under its spell cast

And so I keep walking
Having found a home
In the earth's mind
Where I continue to roam

No mental block
In nature's stream of consciousness
Where I wash my thoughts
And chase the high of its bliss

Journey to Remember When

A stream of consciousness
Runs through the woods
I sit contemplating
The shoulda woulda couldas

Of missing you
Gone too soon
Not enough time to mourn
Leaving loneliness to swoon

No finish line to cross
No closure to speak of
Like a stray cloud in the sky
Or a dove lost above

As I search for peace of mind
Or another piece of your time
Be it laughter and joy
Or sadness's crime

Where I am sentenced
To a lifetime in your eyes
Like a pupil to study
Loss's truths and lies

A fabrication
From the cloth of our love
Cut out for you and I
Custom from the God above

But no
You are not here

Even your tired ghost
Gone and disappeared

And every time
I visit your grave
I think to myself
How soon death you braved

Leaving me here
To count the many ways
How tears trickle down
On my face

As wrinkles appear
On the face of my time
Where death begins to smile
And church bells chime

When I will see you
Once again
And we will both say
Remember when

Flower's Currency

Locked up in a cell
Never found the key to life
Rough childhood
Innocence stolen
By the mature streets
As he ignored the one way signs
To trouble
Father ran away early
His missing love not worthy
For the back of a milk carton
Maybe wearing a serial number
Imprisoned by a first high
As mother tries to unlock
The key to daily hardships
Children suckling from the teat
Of two jobs
Mouths employed by hunger
And the call of the footsteps
Of poverty
To grow rich in want
From between the cracks
A weed crushed by man's sole
Holding a tin cup
Watered by pennies
As the world photosynthesizes
Ways to bloom rich
But the poor rather
The currency of flower petals
Bought by a wind

All in the Timing

What if there was
No such thing as time
And the dew of morning
Hung on just a little while longer
And if it took just a minute
To recall a lifetime of memories
Tick tocking in the subconscious
Where the internal clock blooms
At the root of every feathered call
Of the cuckoo bird
Dawning every hour
To take time under its wing
And fly away to find
Rest in shady thoughts
As clouded minds search
For the increments of day
To count the hand me down past
As we try on the present
Sewing hope and faith
Into the fabric of the future
Wondering if we'll fit
Into the minutes and seconds
Maybe hem the timing
Of my beating heart
When it's always the right time
To love you

Waiting to Go Home

An orphan born
From a crevice of suffering
His parents
Are hopelessness and neglect
His siblings
Hunger and want
Born from the tree of life
But grafted to a dying shrub
His roots can't break through
The hard city concrete
In a metropolis garden
Where a bouquet of city dwellers
Grow all around us
Their spirits blooming
From the cracks in our souls
But we dismiss them
Like weeds without a name
Dismayed that they too
Soak up precious rain
As our clouded thoughts
Remember them late at night
Their eyes and
Their gravitational pull on our peace
As we realize
We are all part
Of the same orphaned world
Waiting to go home

Our Daily Bread

I'm such a quack
Feeding the ducks at the park
Paying my daily bills
Of depression and loneliness
As bread falls like snowflakes
On the lake
With all the nooks and crannies
Of winter
As I look out the window of my mind
Flurries gathering on the windowsill
Of my eyes
And I close the curtains
To my subconscious
Meditate on the feathered wind
Searching for the wings of my soul
As I drop a thought
In the waters of my imagination
Watch it ripple out
Towards the crust of the unknown
Where God feeds man
With the yeast of life
As I rise to His hand
And bite off
More than I can chew
And crumble from heaven
With a heart full of
God's daily bread

Links of Hope

Sin is a prison
From where we sing
In bars of innocence
Out of key
With our shame
With three square meals
Of pride
Served by the devilish warden
Of the world
Where we are sentenced
To guilt's capital punishment
As the faithful hold hands
Like chains to pray for society
Words linking hope
That the Lord
Will free us from
Our solitary confinement
As we speak His name
To unlock our hearts
And we each become
Tiny cells of a living body
Circulating His good word

The Art of Thievery

A masterpiece painting
Succumbs to the art of thievery
Stolen from the corner of the eye
In the priceless night
The moonlight's fingerprints
All over the room
As darkness brushes the world
Searching for the stolen
Piece of truth
A peace of mind robbed
From a thought in time
When the universe aligned
In color and shape
First found hanging
On a wall of the imagination
On the wall of a dream's uterus
Where I too was born in the shades
To steal your stillborn wonders
As I canvass day and night
Searching for the right hour
When your attention drips dry
And I emerge
From the border of darkness
To corner your creation
Into midnight
Leaving only your frame
Of mind
To bristle at the loss

A Love Letter From Mother Nature

The turning of the seasons
Like a page in a love letter
Written from nature to man
Where the sun kisses the earth
At a more intimate degree
And the equator embraces the world
A little tighter … and with more warmth
Where meadows blush
By the touch
Of the spring rain
And the birds and bees
Complement the flowers
To bloom
As Mother Nature
Pollinates my eyes
With its beauty
And my soul begins
To open its petals
Roots finally releasing
From winter's white soil
That held all the colors

Blood in the Rain

Watching the daily news
That channels depression
Names of war torn countries
Love can't pronounce
Lines on a map
Move back and forth
In a game of chess
Where soldiers pick up the check
And mates back home
Wait for their lovers
To cross the frontier
Of the kitchen door
But it's just a window
Of missed opportunity
As on the battlefield
The stars have shrapnelled
In the distance
And the moonlight pierces
The armor of peace
As I change the station
To a nature show
Watch animals hunt one another
Under uniform hunger
As I question man's
Unending appetite
For blood and oil
That don't mix
And the sun charges forth
Gaining ground on our hearts
Crossing all borders
Without a fight
Tries to shed light

On our ignorance
As the rain falls at my window
Like bullets capturing my attention
As a prisoner
Of my own warring nature

Weeding Out the Tears

A bowl of fruit on the table
As the porcelain twilight
Breaks through the glass window
Shining on mother in the kitchen
Plump and pregnant
With the juices of day
As her hands deliver
Morning from the womb of dreams
The sleeping field ripe with dew
Dying fog buried in
Tiny coffins of light
As she begins to feel
Contractions of pain
Nine months of memories
Squeezed into a moment
As a body takes shape
Around a breath
And the world inhales
A new soul
To be fruitful till the
Hyperventilating end
Where God plants our seed
In His garden
Weeding out the sad tears

Devil's Whiskers

The devil snaps his fingers
Sparking a fire
That gets out of hand
As fire trucks close in
In degrees of timing
Flames addressed
To a three decker
Smoke rising
Like hell's ghosts
As the meow of a cat
Claws for oxygen
Her owner burning
To hold her again
As a fireman fights his fear
Hopscotches through the flames
Narrows in on the feline
Counting her nine lives
Whisks her up
And traces his way back
Through the patches of air
Into mother's bosom of safety
Her tears enough
To put out the fires of sadness
As the tail end
Of the devil's plans turn to ash
And life begins to purr
Once again

Dead End Moment

Boy poking around in the woods
With a curious stick
Dead leaves give way
To a body spiritless for days
Clothes torn like
The fabric of the day
The smell of blood
Circulating in the air
The heartbeat of the moment
Pulsing in the veins of the forest
As he wonders
How she reached such a dead end
How the fork in the road
Turned into a knife
Leaving her laying
Spooning with death
As he sits on a rock
Stoned by the vision
So close to death
Never closer
To his own existence
As innocence flatlines
Buried in a nameless grave

Step for Step

And so they dance
A treasured moment
Money can't buy
Their bodies bartering
Back n forth for the moonlight
As she reminisces
On all the silent years
Even without music
Her hand in his
Trusting the tune of their love
Step for step
Through the good times and bad
The melody of the past
Still ringing true into the future
Which may find them
Dancing alone
But even when they are
Face to face with distance
They are always hip
To one another's beat
Hearts always in rhythm
With all the secret notes
Between two bodies

The Earthquake

At first
The glasses started clinking
As if in a toast
To the coming tragedy
And the plates shook
Ready to serve God's wrath
As the bed rocked
In a lullaby bye to the innocent day
And Mother Earth opened her appetite
For destruction and death
At first I thought
It was one of Mother Nature's dreams
As she shifted and rolled in bed
But she was alarmingly awake
Tossing her crust like bedsheets
Wrinkling and tearing
The map beneath our feet
The world's moral compass
Gone awry
As we all rock
In our cradles of fear
Back n forth between
A curse and a prayer
As God lifts his hand
From a vengeful fist
To a welcoming palm
And with a forefinger
Points us towards peace

Crystal Ball

She took a vacation from life
Called in sick
And dialed in to doing nothing
Made herself a tea
As the dawn was brewing
And nothing was stirring
Plopped in at the window
That lets in the eastern light
Opening the curtains
To a new page in her story
Wonders what the author
Has in store
Will she cry again
A river of permanent ink
Or will he pencil in love
Easily erased by the first tear
She feels so small
Just a side character in a romance novel
In a plot that goes nowhere
But she will continue
Reading her future
Until she stares into
The depths of the final period
Looking into a crystal ball

Shards of the Future

She looks down at the crystal ball
From above as if
Looking down on the earth
Parting the lady's cloudy future
With her hands
Careful not to touch
The world reflecting
Beneath the glass
Something not alive
But not dead
As of a relic from
An alien purgatory
As she leans over the
Unworldly orb
Her eyes reading the
Trapped ghosts
Repeating a gypsy prayer
That brings it to life
A world beginning to stir
And boiling over into visions
As the woman listens
To heartbreak and dismay
Her emotions cracking on
The surface
Breaking out into tears
Such passion from the past
Cracking the molded destiny
As shards of glass cut into fate
And distort the future

The Cornerstone

They immigrated to the U.S.
To find borders
That hold in the peace
No more boundaries
To practice their religion
Crossed the seas
Between the pews of waves
With their altars in their hearts
The scent of frankincense
They exhaled on sure ground
Making sure their prayers
Didn't get lost
In the translation to the generations
As they built churches
In corners they were driven to
With the cornerstone of faith
Smuggled over in the soul
Erecting crosses to cross
Over the ages
As believers lean against
The brick and mortar of hope
While word by word
Society builds a Babel of sin
For a crumbling future

An Arresting Dream

Dawn
Simple as dew
Complex as
A conversation about a dream
But what did you really see there
Between the loose ends of sleep
That tied you up in knots
To unravel in an early morning talk
With a lover
Unpacking your words
And all their luggage
Into a cup of coffee
Having crossed the borders of night
Into the safe checkpoint of his arms
His eyes patting you down
From the sharp worries of the world
That may prick your love
As his arresting smile
Handcuffs the darkness
Finding you guilty of innocence
And sentences you
To a lifetime
Behind bars of his love poems

Fishing

He got there early
To start fishing
Baiting the sun
From the horizon
As he reeled in the light
Dropping in his squirming hopes
That ripple to the edge of his patience
But all he catches
Is empty time on his hands
A tall tale
Without a hook or ending
As the hours
Scale the day
And he pulls in his line
From the drowning afternoon
As the moon worms its way up
And the moonlight hooks him
As he sinks into the depths
Of the rocking night

Hormones of Morning

A child
In the sunrise of his life
Leaving the horizon
Of mother's lap
Into the maturing hours
As a young girl's love
Dawns on his darkness
And she shows him the real
Stars of passion glistening
On her skin
Wiping moonlight
From one another's bodies
As they sail on smiles
Towards the shores of twilight
Where the sun comes of age
At the speed of a heart's beat
And the hormones of morning
Are pollinated

Closet Where Seasons Keep Their Junk

In the closet
Where seasons keep their junk
Autumn stores its leaves
In a box like
So many playing cards
With a number
For every shade of orange
And winter dries its icicles
Dripping from clothes hangers
Just above
The dark cold corner
Where the year hides its
Christmas gifts of snow
Wrapped in dust
Behind spring
Waiting on a shelf
To fall on my head
With its torrential rain
As I search the pockets
Of my favorite pair of shorts
For a dollar or two
To bribe the summer
To stay a bit longer
As I turn the handle
Of my mind
Closing the door
To so many doors
Look out the window
Enjoy the sun
Part the cloth clouds
As it hangs
From a hook in the sky

Rubble of Dreams

What if it was all a dream
A life in a bed of fantasy
Reality resting
On a pillow of lullabies
A sleepy song threaded
Between the eyes
Of life and death
Composed by the imagination
Where you are the band
Of your instrumental senses
As you wake
From surreal to surreal
Your mind clutching
At disappearing images
Like quickly skimming a poem
Without beginning or end
Your eyes burning bridges
From syllable to syllable
As you swing from word to word
From belief to belief
Turning the pages
That crumble like walls
As you rise
From the rubble of visions

Blind Date

He waits for his
Blind date at the bar
Hopefully a Mona Lisa
And not a homely Felicia
It's getting late
And a small buzz starts
To take up the place
Or is it just in his head
From the three dirty martinis
With an olive drowning
Like him in the spirit of the night
As an angel
Opens the earthly door
Her head on a swivel
For warm eyes
Between the cold shoulders
As I raise my hand
And put up a smile
Like a lighthouse of hope
In the sea of faces
As I wave her in
From the high tide of strangers
To the shores of my arms
And she turns from a blind date
Into a heavenly vision

A Man's Hands

A man's hands tell a lot
Veins of blood bulging
Hard as a frozen river
But tender enough to flow
Over a woman's shoulder

Rooted in the earth enough
To chop wood
But delicate as a wind
To pluck a flower

He's held mother's hand
To cross the streets of innocence
And from his same hand
Learned from father
To wipe sweat from his brow

From God he's studied
How to knock on the door of want
And bring idle hands together
In prayer's workshop

As a babe they blindly hover
And squeeze mother's teat
For milk the shade of dawn
And in old age they clutch
A cane from a dying tree
To walk with time's
Shaky legs

Hands can count
Your many lovers

You have separated from
Like lonely fingers
Or brought together
To squeeze out
Every drop of moonlight
As I make a fist
Like a beating heart
To fight the dying pulse of night

A Woman's Hands

A woman's hands
Hold the teat of Mother Nature
Feeding a wind
That swirls in the meadows
Writing love letters
In invisible ink

They pray the rosary
Among a garden of roses
Plucking black petals for those lost
And red for those
Still rooted in life's passion

And they cook
With love's perfect recipe
And bandage the bruises
That have cut into life

They read a bedtime story
To the child's imagination
Bidding bon voyage
To his dreams

Caressingly drive a man crazy
As he begs to hold them
To close around his loneliness
And wear a diamond
That rings true

They are made to count
Her many moods
The lazy stem of afternoon

That blooms from morning
And the spirit of night
Where fire and wine foreshadow
Bodies' burning of one flame

As she opens her palm
To be read by the moonlight
And it quickly closes around me
Keeping me from her future
As I take a backroad
To the corner
Of her eyes
Where I hitchhike
To reach her smile

Water's Journey

Goes
From cage to cage
Always looking
To release its cells
As it makes a break
By its own nature
To a river or stream
Where I wash my face
In its glittering journey
Before it has visions
Of greater things
Like an ocean
That waves it in
To graduate
Into the ebb and flow
Of so many
Creatures and callings

Like telling schools of stories
To seashells and bottles
Pearls of words that
Put them to sleep
On a bed of sand

Where I am beached from life
Walk the shore listening
To all the world's conversations
Wash up at the sole of my feet
Feel the gravitational pull
Of their worries
Like tiny boats sinking
As they grab for my breath

To stay afloat
But I must let them go
Before their stormy waters
Part toward me
And the captain of my tears
Steers my way
Shipwrecking in my eyes

Heaven To Look Forward To

Well there's heaven to look forward to
When your favorite poem
No longer rhymes with your life
And your fave album skips a beat
Leaving you out of the groove
And your go to book
No longer binds you to its ending

Well there's heaven to look forward to
When the mirror starts
Telling lies to your face
And old age reflects
From the surface of a sunset
Your cane barely holding up
A shaky future

But there's always her smile
That never dies from her face
And the fireworks of freckles
Blushing on her cheeks
From where I rise
To her heavenly blue eyes
The only afterlife
I need

Gears of Loss

I boarded the train
As the gears of missing you
Began to churn
And the steam of loneliness
Filled the sky
As I filled a front seat
Elbow to elbow with your memories
In the back of my mind
Like luggage I had to leave behind

As the faces begin to puzzle me
A familiar smile… a warm gaze
Pieces I bristle together
On the canvas in my mind
As an image of you
Steals in
From the borders of distance
And I brush up
With your ghost
And wonder with what color
To paint our love
Maybe black for heartbreak
Or red for the moments of passion
An innocent baby blue
For the child that didn't make it
Birthing pastels
For all your shady moods of loss
That drove me to leave

As the soulless
Metal machine reaches its destination
My past grinding to a halt
But I'm still traveling
Towards a virgin white space
That has yet to be painted

Winter Worries

The complaints accumulated
With every flake
As the clouds slipped
Into the slit of an objection box
In the horizon
Signed by our worries
But father always
Held his tongue
Never scribbled on the X
With frozen ink
It was his favorite season
Something about falling
Hopeless white fragments
Of a life that came together in the end
And disappeared into the sun's forgiveness
That gave him strength
But he was outnumbered
By the rising colorful voices
Of spring flowers
Each petal a vote in the wind
That called for the felling
Of old man winter's head
As the rains roll in
And father's quill
Unwillingly flows... like an icicle melting
Signing the season's death certificate

Haiku 1

The lie detector
Fizzles burns out reading your
Mysterious eyes

Haiku 2

A phlebotomist
Medical world's vampire
With vial habit

Haiku 3

Took bite out of time
Trip to the dreaded dentist
A close brush with pain

Haiku 4

She's leaving him be
Luggage packed ticket bought she
Pilots destiny

Haiku 5

Letter in mailbox
Addressed to a broken heart
Love's destiny sealed

Haiku 6

When the early day
Is first learning how to talk
Night speaks its last words

Haiku 7

Raining cats and dogs
Sheltered neighborhood listens
To the night's tall tales

Haiku 8

Take afternoon nap
Crossing weary bridge with dreams
Before it crumbles

Haiku 9

Yes it's my birthday
Candles spilling off the edge
But flame is dimming

Haiku 10

Snow's many chapters
In winter's long drawn novel
Edited by sun

Haiku 11

Shades of gang colors
Graffitied on ghetto walls
Something to live for

Haiku 12

Mother giving birth
Pain and anguish of labor
Cry born from a cry

Haiku 13

Everyday I push
The poetic envelope
Addressed to your heart

Haiku 14

Million butterflies
Resting on the trunks of trees
Slowly chip like bark

Haiku 15

Quite windy last night
As if ghosts were being whipped
Calm day heals all scars

Haiku 16

Snow angel on ground
Lifts its wings and takes to sky
Children's cold hearts melt

Haiku 17

The cable is out
So I turn to the window
Watch nature channel

Haiku 18

Crazy about you
My heart in a straight jacket
Committed to love

Haiku 19

Sharp spine of sand dune
Shifts in the wind like a snake
Molting sun's shadows

Haiku 20

Hit my funny bone
Painful joke creator made
Mean sense of humor

Haiku 21

I smoke cigarette
Or is it smoking me as
I filter the thought

Haiku 22

They dance the tango
Saturday night's bold rhythm
Hand on moonlight's hip

Haiku 23

Eating cereal
Letters spell out good morning
Chew over moment

Made in the USA
Middletown, DE
04 June 2025